CW00406676

Costa Rica Travel Guide

The Top 10 Highlights in Costa Rica

Table of Contests

Introduction to Costa Rica

When you think of a perfect exotic vacation Coast Rica is definitely among the first destinations which come to mind. With wide incredible beaches, beautiful wilderness and warm locals, this tiny Central American country is the perfect summer destination, except, thanks to its location, summer is always here.

Coast Rica means "Rich Coast" in Spanish and the name is truly fitting. Barley populated before the 16th century, this country was under the Spanish rule for 300 hundreds years before the country became independent. Soon Costa Rica transformed into one of the richest countries in Latin America.

Thanks to its ideal location between the Pacific Ocean and the Caribbean Sea, Costa Rica boasts a tropical weather year round which makes it a true paradise every day of the year. However, the beautiful wilderness doesn't attract just vacationers in search of a good time, but also conservationists and outdoors enthusiasts who love to explore the biodiversity of this country's tropical forests. Costa Rica is also a paradise for avid birdwatchers with over 800 species of birds living here year-round. In fact Costa Rica has 5 percent of the biodiversity of the entire world.

Thrill seekers also love to spend their vacations here because of the numerous opportunities for windsurfing, rafting, scuba diving and many more water sports that can be either practiced or learned here.

One of the best ways to visit this beautiful country is by taking the bus or just biking. Though you should take some precautions when using the public transportation system, it is one of the easiest ways to make sure you see everything.

Costa Rica is also the meeting point between South American culture, pre-Colombian traditions and European influences which means every city and village is filled with funky festivals, great cuisine and lively nightlife.

San Jose, the capital, is also the largest and most populous city in Costa Rica, with about half of the country's population living here. The rest of cities are mostly little former fishing villages or tiny cities secluded in the lush jungle.

Costa Rica is also home of dozens of volcanos, six of which are still active. Which means this beautiful country is also the perfect destination for geologist or simply for tourists who love to discover craters and learn more about volcanoes.

All in all, this breath taking country is an ideal destination for any type of tourists, from thrill seeker, to lazy ones who just want to relax by the beach. What is more, the topical weather makes this country and excellent vacation spot any day of the year.

1. San Jose

The capital city of Costa Rica is the perfect spot to start your journey. Here tourists get a taste of Costa Rican culture form interesting museums to beautiful parks and plenty of street artists. This city is also the best spot to indulge in some retail therapy in stylish boutiques spread throughout the city.

San Jose is hidden in the Central Valley and is the perfect place to escape the tropical weather. Here the temperatures are a lot cooler so tourists usually love to spend a few days here just to escape the torrid heat.

The heart and soul of the city is right on Avendia Central where you'll find some of the most fancy restaurants and high end boutiques in town. From there on tourists flock to Plaza de la Culture, the actual center of the city. Keep in mind that San Jose is not exactly a metropolis so it will not keep you busy for long, even if it's the largest city in Costa Rica.

But that shouldn't discourage you from visiting it. San Jose still has several treasures just waiting to be discovered. Like the National Theatre, probably the most recognized building in the entire city. Over a century old, the true beauty of this building is hidden inside. From the outside it looks remarkably uninteresting, but once you step foot inside you'll find ceilings covered in gold, marble staircases and exquisite decorations. So don't be fooled by the unimaginative exterior.

What is more, San Jose has several incredible theatres, most of them being the main touristic attractions. Whether you simply want to visit the European style buildings or even take in a show, these theaters should be on your must-see list. Apart from the National Theatre, tourists love to discover Melic Salazar Theatre or Tetra Variegates, the oldest one in the city.

The capital of Costa Rica also houses plenty of museums for curious minds, from the Children's Museums to the Pre-Colombian Gold Museum which is located under the Plaza de la Culture. The latter boasts over 1.600 artefacts, some dating back to AD 500.

Architecture buffs have to visit the Blue Castle, an incredible neoclassical residential house built over a century ago. Initially the house was built for a famous politician and it was used by various parliament members and presidents throughout its history. The building is known for the intricate detailing on its façade. Legend says the name of this house comes from the fact that it used to have a blue tinted glass dome right on top, which was destroyed in the 20's.

San Jose also boasts several beautiful churches and temples, but, by far the most impressive one is the Metropolitan Cathedral. This church used to be a small chapel made out of mud with straw roof. But throughout the years it was turned into a massive cathedral with huge columns and several additional chapels built around it.

Since San Jose is located in a wide valley surrounded by volcanos and mountains, it's no wonder that this city has several large urban parks. La Sabena Metropolitan Park is the largest one and the most visited. After discovering San Jose's beautiful buildings and very intriguing museums, the best place to decompress and take in the fresh air is this over 178 acres large urban park. The origins of this park date back to over two centuries ago and throughout the time the park's flora was enriched with the help of locals who love planting new species here. The park also houses several artificial lakes, a stadium and an Art Museum perfect for a day of leisure.

Finally, the actual flavor of the city is encompassed into the main produce market, Mercado Central, an eclectic mix of every aspect of this community's culture and traditions. Here tourists get a unique insight into the daily lives of locals, as well as a great opportunity to try some of the traditional cuisine.

2. Adrenal Volcano

Adrenal Volcano is a true symbol of Costa Rica and one of the most visited landmarks in the entire country. Despite the fact that Costa Rica has dozens of volcanos and six of them are still active. Adrenal is located inside a National Park with the same name, about 90 kilometers from the capital of San Jose. The actual mountain is over 1,600 meters high and on top tourists get to admire a 140 meters wide crater. The main focus of this area is, of course, the volcano, but the national park also houses many other treasures. Costa Rica has a very rich biodiversity, and about 70 percent of all animal species in this country can be spotted in this park. The area also has a very rich fauna with many plant species that can only be found in this place.

The volcano is considerably young according to specialists who managed to date its activity back to about 7,500 years ago. However, since 2010, Adrenal has entered in its resting phase. That doesn't mean that it's still not a beautiful sight. Its proportions are very symmetric offering visitors a perfect sight no matter the place they choose to admire it.

The entire area was mostly unknown until the 30's when a group of explorers managed to reach the summit. Since then, there were several eruptions recorded, the most serious being the first one. In 1968, Adrenal erupted suddenly, killing dozens of people and burring three villages in ash.

Today, Arenal is a magnet for volcanos enthusiasts and outdoorsmen who love to explore the tropical forest around it. Those who are athletic enough can hike their way to the summit and discover a breathtaking view of the entire Alajuela province.

Not too far from Arenal National Park, tourists can also explore the Venado Caves, a string of caves with many treasures just waiting to be discovered. Inside, among the stalactites and stalagmites refreshing subterranean streams have colorful fishes swimming and transparent frogs clinging to the rocks around it. Some caves even house several colonies of bats.

The park is surrounded by a few tiny cities and villages but, by far the most beautiful one, that must be visited, is La Fortuna. The name of this city is closely related with the Arenal Volcano. When it erupted in 1968, the lava and the ash spread on the western side of the mountain, while this city was on the eastern side. Since that day the city, which used to be called El Borio, changed its name into La Fortuna ("the Fortunate").

Usually, tourists who plan on visiting the volcano start their journey here. In La Fortuna there are a number of organized tours which lead visitors among the most important trails through the park. The most beloved attraction here is actually about 5 kilometers outside of the city – a 75 meters drop waterfall right at the base of another dormant volcano, Chato. La Fortuna Waterfall is fed by Tenorio River and, usually, adventurous tourists hike down the waterfall and swim in the natural pool formed at the bottom.

3. Tamarindo

One of the most beautiful beaches in the entire Costa Rica is in the village of Tamarindo. Usually this tiny village has about 500 locals, but during the touristic season there are 100 times more people, thanks to thousands of tourists who love to spend their vacation here.

Tamarindo is a staple for Costa Rica's best features from wide beaches by the Pacific Ocean to warm locals and breath taking surrounding landscapes. However, if you want to experience the true Costa Rican lifestyle, then Tamarindo is not the best choice. Thanks to the beauty of this region, it's also the most popular city in the country, which means that at any given time Tamarindo is swarmed by tourists, which makes it a lot more difficult to experience the city's true flavor. The largest crowds gather during the high season between December and May.

Tamarindo Beach is the epitome of paradise – an over 3 kilometers long beach surrounded by national parks and high mountains. The water is a perfect shade of light blue and visitors get a sneak peek into the incredible fauna hidden in the tropical forest right from their loungers. Howler monkeys and parakeets can be spotted while sunbathing, and the northern part of the beach is also the place where Leatherback Turtles lay their eggs. Every time they hatch visitors get to experience the incredible spectacle of tiny turtles making their way to the water.

The beautiful ocean is also a magnet for surfers and professional fishermen. The currents can be pretty strong but the water is perfect for surfers of any level. Tourists also love practicing scuba diving, snorkeling, jet skiing and kayaking.

Thanks to its increasing popularity, Tamarindo has developed just like most seaside resorts with expensive hotels and restaurant, but also with plenty of surfing school. The city's nightlife also caters mostly to the richest tourists who love to spend their nights in one of the fancy night clubs right on the beach.

But that doesn't mean the Tamarindo is a destination just for deep-pocketed tourists. There are plenty to do with a low budget from sunbathing on one of the most beautiful beaches in the world to discovering the tropical forest around and the largest mangrove estuary in Central America which happens to be near this city.

4. Puerto Viejo de Talamanca

Among all the beautiful places in Costa Rica where surfers gather in search for the perfect wave, Puerto Viejo de Talamanca is by far the most popular and beloved. On the shore of the Caribbean Sea, this coastal town makes a stark contrast with the more fashionable Tamarindo. Here most visitors are backpackers and surfers, which mean this tiny village has a very relaxed and laid-back atmosphere. The natural beauty of this area has attracted curious visitors for decades, but, despite that, the former fishing village has maintained most of its unique charm.

Puerto Viejo is surrounded by tropical forests and thanks to its location on the Caribbean Coast, it rains quite often which makes the flora even lusher. There isn't much to do here but enjoy the black and white sand beaches which extend for dozens of kilometers. Round Puerto Viejo there are several smaller villages that are also worth seeing, in order to get a closer look into the true Costa Rican lifestyle. Make sure you rent a bike rather than a car because the roads are practically made out of potholes.

Nature enthusiasts have the perfect spot to start discovering the incredible wilderness in the jungle just a few steps outside Puerto Viejo.

Those who want to catch a glimpse of one of the most reclusive cats in this area must visit the Jaguar Rescue Center, outside Puerto Viejo. This non-profit foundation's main purpose is to recover any animals that are brought here from local communities. Don't expect to see prides of jaguars as soon as you enter the center. Most animals are rereleased into the wild as soon as they are taken care of. You'll be able to take a tour of the entire area and even pet baby sloth or baby howler monkeys.

Puerto Viejo is mostly famous for its Salsa Brava waves, which means most tourists are here for surfing or for admiring professional athletes. That is why, the quiet former fishing village turned into a mecca for surfers form every corner of the world.

5. Tortuguero National Park

Though it's one of the most remote parks in Costa Rica, Tortuguero National Park is also one of the most visited one. Accessible only by boat or plane, the park is located not too far from Puerto Viejo.

This is also one of the few areas where walking is actually discouraged. The best way to explore this incredible park is by boat and the only mark trails are along the beach where tourists can spot turtle nests.

This jungle is a true paradise for any conservationists and outdoor enthusiast. This area is a true meeting point for fresh water and the sea, making the canals, beaches and lagoons a perfect home for tens of thousands of species of animals, fishes and plants.

Some of the strangest but also rare species of reptiles and birds live here. Actually, the park houses about over 300 species of birds, about 100 species of reptiles and many more mammals.

As tourists explore the wilderness, they will get a unique chance to come in close contact with a large number of animals and reptiles.

The name Tortuguero means turtle catcher so it's no wonder the main attraction of this national park is the turtle colonies. Dozens of species nest on the beaches of this park, and some of them are near extinction due to hunters. A group of scientists started a conservation program for sea turtles in this park and the program is still functioning to this day with significant results. It's important to know that tourists are not allowed on the beach after 6 pm unaccompanied. At night, visitors who want to catch a glimpse of baby turtles hatching and making their way to the sea, must hire a local guide, because this area is protected.

Tortuguero National Park is also a very popular destination for bird watchers. Hundreds of bird species can be observed among the canals or between the hundreds-year old trees in the jungle, from colorful toucans and peacocks to large macaws and parrots. Moreover, one of the largest and most dangerous mammals hidden in the jungle is the jaguar, but it' quite difficult to spot one. The waters are also populated by thousands and thousands of colorful fishes, alongside manatees, crocodiles and fin whales.

Near the park a small village located on a sand bar is the closest inhabited place to this secluded area. The village of Tortuguero, right on the Northern Caribbean coast, is the perfect place to start your unforgettable journey through the park. Though the beaches here are truly idyllic, the village is not exactly the perfect place for swimming. The currents are very strong, while the canals nearby are infested with crocodiles. In fact each year there are several cases in which disoriented tourists drowned or were killed by crocodiles, because their fishing boats flipped over.

6. Montezuma

Located right on the tip of Nicoya Peninsula, Montezuma is a former fishing village that has gained in popularity in the last few decades thanks to its exquisite beaches and beautiful surroundings. This town is the cheaper version of Tamarindo but that doesn't mean it's not equally striking. There are several waterfalls in the surrounding areas, while the Cabo Blanco Natural Reserve offers tourists the opportunity to discover a little part of Costa Rica's wilderness.

The village also houses a very well-known yoga community and a famous film festival. But the main attractions are, of course, the beaches. Here they are a lot more secluded, and the village itself doesn't offer more than a few souvenir shops and hotels. Though it is a popular touristic destination, Montezuma managed to keep its rural charm for which it became popular in the first place.

That is why apart from sun bathing and discovering the wilderness around, there aren't that many things to do. Tourists can rent a horse and take horseback trips through the forests or they can explore the three waterfalls near the village. Though the area is quite beautiful, the best part here is the opportunity to swim in the crystal clear waters of the natural pools formed at the bottom of these falls.

Despite the fact that there aren't many shops in the village, there are a few boutiques where tourists can buy souvenirs and most of the streets of Montezuma are lined with street vendors offering some of the most interesting and quirkiest objects from strange looking masks to handmade clothes and jewelry.

At night the city comes to life with music and people dancing in the street. This tiny village has a very close-knit community and it's very easy to experience the true Caribbean lifestyle down to the cuisine and delicious cocktails.

All in all, Montezuma is the perfect choice for a few days of relaxation on one of the many secluded and untouched beaches or even for a destination wedding.

7. Monteverde Reserve

Near the Cordillera de Tilaran mountain range tourists will get the chance to discover another breathtaking park with over 26,000 acres of cloud forest. The Monteverde Reserve is one of the most popular cloud forest in the world with over 2,500 of plant species and hundreds of animals and reptiles.

Just like most natural parks in Costa Rica, the Monteverde Reserve is a true paradise for any tourist who loves nature and wilderness.

Back in the 50's a group of Quakers left the United States of America and settled in these cloud forests where they started building a peaceful and simple life. Some of the families who took refuge here actually established this reserved. The Quakers were the ones who named this area Monteverde meaning the Green Mountain. Not long after the reserve was established, tourists begun to take notice of this incredible corner of the world. Thanks to its rich biodiversity, this area became a magnet for scientists and conservationists who made serious efforts in order to protect this region. Though the number of foreign tourists rose ten times, the area is still perfectly maintained by a number of researchers. Nowadays, over 70,000 de visitors come here every year in order to explore one of the few untouched corners of the world.

The entire reserve has several trails, some easier to cross than other. Most of them are less than 1 kilometer long and take less than an hour to complete. The longest one, however, is El Camino ("The Road"), a 2 kilometer long trail perfect for bird watching or discovering butterflies. There are also canopy tours and suspension bridges that will make your trip even more exciting. Zip-lining is also a great way to discover this park. Though the reserve can be quite interesting to explore alone, those who don't have a lot of experience should definitely hire one of the many guided tours.

Most visitors choose to stay overnight in the little village of Santa Elena not too far from Monteverde Reserve, but those who want to spend more time in the jungle can sleep in one of the many lodges built throughout the park. In fact, this area has one of the best examples of sustainable tourism in the world.

Over 2 percent of the biodiversity of the Earth can be found in the Monteverde Reserve. More than 100 species of mammals live in theses woods including monkeys, different types of cats and sloths, alongside tens of thousands of insects and about 5,000 species of moths. The reserve is also home to more than 1,200 species of amphibians and reptiles including venomous snakes and frogs.

Another great attraction of this park is the fact that visitors are able to literally step on the Continental divide, the line between the Caribbean side and the Pacific side. This is probably the most photographed area as tourists love to take photos of themselves form on side to the other.

8. Dominical

Another popular destination among surfers is the small town of Dominical. A former fishing village, Dominical has gained popularity in the past few years also thanks to its wide beaches and great waves.

Dominical is located on the Pacific coast, in the southern area of Costa Rica and, as most touristic villages, it's dedicated entirely to beach enthusiasts.

Surfers love this village thanks to its consistent waves which makes this one of the best places for practicing but also learning this exciting sport. Depending how well you can stay up on the board, you can choose among several beaches around Dominical. All of them are wide, virtually untouched and also perfect for sunbathing. Swimming however is strongly discouraged as the riptides here can be very strong.

The most popular beach is Playa Dominicalito, south of the village, and is the perfect place for tourists who want to learn how to surf. Here the lush nature merges with the sky-blue waters in a breathtaking landscape. Further south, at Punta Dominical, the shore is more rugged and it's the ideal spot to simply watch the ocean's waves just break over the rocks.

As like many other Costa Rican villages, Dominical is surrounded by lush jungle just waiting to be discovered. There are also several waterfalls nearby that are worth visiting, like Nauyaca Waterfalls, where tourists can finally take a swim.

Since the main activity here is surfing, it's no wonder the town's atmosphere is laid-back and very relaxed. Don't expect a wide variety of shops and fancy hotels. Most tourists choose one of the sustainable lodges built not too far from the beach.

Those who want to take their first lessons in surfing or scuba diving this is definitely the perfect spot for them. There are a number of schools who offer classes in several languages.

Dominical is very close to the Marino Ballena National Park, so visitors often get to spot whales right form the shores of the village. Nearby, another popular attraction is Parque Reptilandia, a medium size reserve with many species of snakes and frogs as well as crocodiles and a Komodo Dragon, which can be closely admired by brave visitors.

Just like many other coastal towns, the main highlight of the local cuisine is fresh seafood. Here restaurants welcome tourists with traditional dishes that combine the Caribbean flavor with Latin influences. What is more, the ingredients used are always fresh and locally resourced.

9. Osa Peninsula

In the Southern region of Cost Rica, not too far from the Panama border, the Osa Peninsula welcomes tourists with incredible wilderness and towns surrounded by legends with pirates and treasures. This is the wildest area in the entire country, and since we're talking about Costa Rica that's worth something.

Bird watchers flock in this peninsula in order to discover some of the most magnificent bird species in Costa Rica. This area is the most popular among bird enthusiasts on the entire Pacific Coats of Central America. In fact, Osa houses half of the species that are living in the entire country.

About one third of the entire peninsula is covered by the protected rainforest of Corcovado National Park. Most of the areas here are untouched by humans and are home to many endangered species like tapirs and jaguars.

Since this is one of the most secluded regions in the entire Costa Rica, it's pretty challenging to find lodging here, but every hotel and bungalow built in the area is completely sustainable. In fact, this is one of the best eco-tourism regions in the entire Central America.

Tourists who dare to venture outside the more popular regions will discover here an untouched wonderland of animals and exotic plants. They'll have the opportunity to explore one of the most secluded and wild places on Earth, and spot where reclusive animals like pumas, jaguars, harpy eagles, armadillos and several species of monkeys live. Also, the Osa Peninsula is home to the deadliest snake in Costa Rica – the Fer-de-lance, which can be very aggressive if disturbed. As with most national parks in this country, the best way to explore this rain forest and also make sure you don't get lost is by hiring a guide. That way you'll get to see every part of this peninsula that's worth exploring but also learn more about the fascinating biodiversity here.

The majority of tourists start their trip in the village of Puerto Jimenez, a former gold mine town, or in Drake Bay, named after the infamous British pirate Sir Francis Drake, who actually discovered this town. Legend says he buried his treasure on the beaches of this charming city in 1579. That is why Puerto Jimenez attracts many visitors who try to find the famed treasure on the wide beaches of this idyllic town.

Just off the Osa Peninsula, tourists with a taste for the mysterious travel to Isla del Cano, a small island mostly famous for its stone spheres. Also known as the Diquis Spheres, they are thought to be created by the now extinct Diquis culture, which dates back to 600 AD. They were found in the Diquis Delta in the 30's and since then many theories have circulated around them regarding their origin and purpose.

There are dozens of spheres raging from a few centimeters to over 2 meters in diameter. There are several legends that talk about how these mysterious spheres got there, including the fact that they were made by nature or that they came from Atlantis. Some claimed the spheres are perfectly rounded, though some differ in diameter. They are all displayed in situ and can be visited at any time, along some other remains of this fascinating culture.

10. San Gerardo de Dota

Not too far from the capital of San Jose, the sleepy village of San Gerardo de Dota is the perfect place to discover how local farmers live in Costa Rica. This very little town hidden in the Los Quetzales National Park is also extremely popular among birdwatchers because this is the primary habitat for the resplendent Quetzal, the most famous bird in the country.

San Gerardo de Dota is a more peaceful alternative to other villages in the cloud forest area of Costa Rica. From this secluded spot tourists embark into a once in a lifetime trip through some of the oldest forests in the world. The village has plenty of sustainable lodges where visitors can spend the night. San Gerardo de Dota is also not too far from the Cerro de la Muerte, the highest point of the Inter-American Highway, fitly named the "Mountain of Death". This peek reaches the elevation of 3,451 meters and offers brave visitors breathtaking views of the entire area. The highway basically divides the Cordillera de Talamanca mountain range and is the best options for tourists which choose to drive through these parts.

However, San Gerardo de Dota is mostly a paradise for bird enthusiasts since here they can discover hundreds of species from hummingbirds to woodpeckers and, of course, the quetzals. These striking birds can be spotted most of the year, particularly during mating season in April and May.

This tiny village also houses a farming community perfect for fishermen who can catch trout, either fly fishing or lure fishing.

Since San Genaro de Dota is at over 2.200 meters above the sea level, the air and climate here is quite different from most towns in Coast Rica. Which means the weather can be quite cold, and not at all similar to the torrid weather on both coasts. Though most tourists, when planning a trip to this magnificent country, don't think of hiking through the mountain range, San Genaro de Dota is a beautiful surprise for those bold enough to venture through these parts.

Printed in Great Britain
by Amazon.co.uk, Ltd.,
Marston Gate.